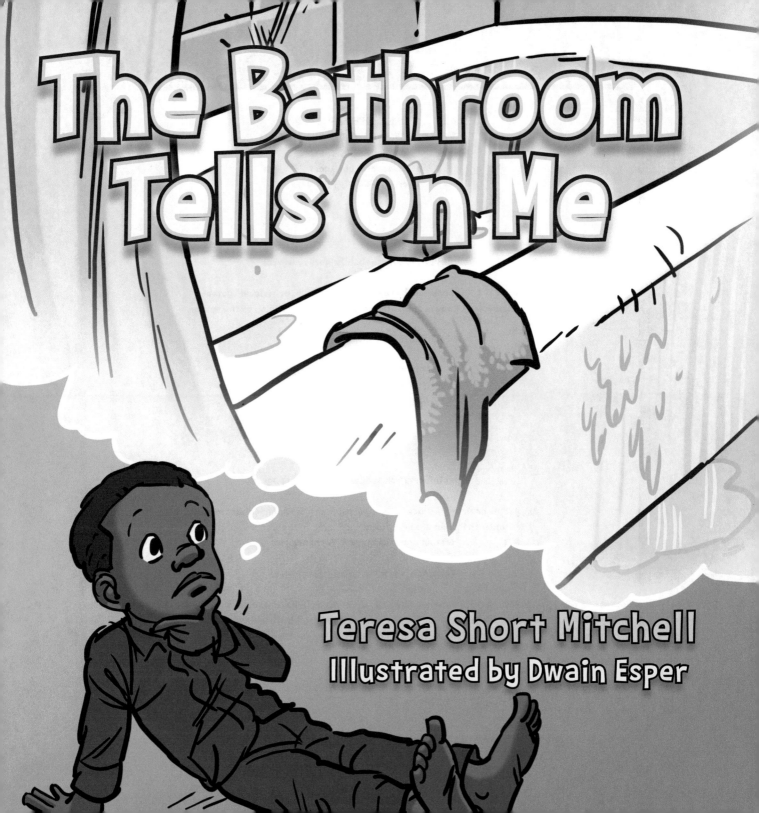

The Bathroom Tells On Me

Teresa Short Mitchell

Illustrated by Dwain Esper

AuthorHouse™
1663 Liberty Drive
Bloomington, IN 47403
www.authorhouse.com
Phone: 1 (800) 839-8640

Published by AuthorHouse 10/25/2018

ISBN: 978-1-4969-0556-7 (sc)
ISBN: 978-1-5462-3584-2 (hc)
ISBN: 978-1-4969-0559-8 (e)

Library of Congress Control Number: 2014907038

authorHOUSE®

This book has been written for all the parents and grandparents who are trying to teach and instill cleanliness values in their children and grandchildren.

Special thanks to my daughter, Latrese and her son, Brian who inspired me to take this book from my mind and bring it to life.

"Young man, I want you to go and take your bath and get ready for bed," Grandma says in a firm voice.

Then added, "For the record, son, I know exactly what I said."

Brian gets up and slowly walks across the floor.

When he goes into the bathroom,
Grandma says, "Close the door."

3

Brian thinks, then says to himself, "Oooooh, she's so mean!"

When he comes out, he says, "Look Grandma, I'm so fresh and so clean!"

Grandma looks at him and gives him a smile.

"You do look fresh and clean child. Now, come and sit by me for a while."

5

Brian responds, "But Grandma, I did what you said, I took a bath and got ready for bed."

"It is okay son, I just want to see, if you really have been listening to me."

Brian sits down on the floor, where he had sat many nights before.

Grandma says, "You know I can tell if you have brushed your teeth."

7

"I know, Grandma because the bathroom tells on me."

Brian begins to really think, "Did I remember to clean the sink?"

While Brian is thinking, Grandma asks, "Did you remember to clean the tub?"

"I bought a new cleaner so you don't have to scrub."

Grandma is playing the question game.

Every night the questions are the same.

Grandma asks, "If you know all that, why are we still having this chat?"

Brian drops his head and begins to cry, but not one tear fell from either eye.

"Son, I am not being mean. I can only go by what I have seen."

"Do you remember what I taught you about the toilet seat?"

Brian puts his head in his hands and says,
"The bathroom is going to tell on me."

15

"It sounds like the bathroom and
I would like to thank you."

17

Directions: Match the mood/feeling word on the left with its facial expression on the right.

HAPPY

EMBARRASSED

ANGRY (MAD)

SAD

CONFUSED

Directions: Match rhyming words by drawing a line from each word on the left to a word on the right.

game	smile
see	door
scrub	that
think	do
mean	same
while	me
you	tub
chat	clean
door	sink

ACTIVITY SHEET

created by Teresa Short Mitchell, 2015
Book signings/events: 678.572.5952

Book selected top 8 out of 15,000 by Authorhouse Publishing

Directions: Find and circle each word below.

BATHROOM	FLOOR	TEACH
BRIAN	GRANDMA	TEACH
CLEAN	RESPECT	TELLS
DOOR		

S	E	H	T	O	L	C	W	G	R
A	Z	T	K	R	T	A	B	L	F
U	R	E	S	P	E	C	T	F	L
F	L	E	I	G	V	T	C	L	O
B	A	T	H	R	O	O	M	O	O
R	X	E	O	A	G	R	T	U	R
I	D	A	L	N	F	O	E	R	D
A	H	C	K	D	L	N	L	K	O
N	O	H	E	M	Z	Q	L	C	O
M	C	L	E	A	N	X	S	B	R

Directions: Show you know the difference. Write the word respect or responsible for each sentence below.

_____ Not talking back to adults.

_____ Doing your homework on time.

_____ Cleaning up after yourself.

_____ Holding the door for an older person.

18

MORE ABOUT THE AUTHOR

Mine is really simple. I ask for everything I want, need and desire. If I get it, then I am better off and it is a wonderful thing. If I do not, then I am no worse off than I was before I asked. (As an educator, I know that is a double negative). Basically, my position can only improve.

PHILOSOPHY OF EDUCATION

Children are our future. We must plan and invest in our future. This means we must invest in children at an early age. The way I view it, we can invest in them with money, time, energy, understanding, love and education while they are young or continue to invest in more prisons, social dependency and societal fear as they grow older.

COMMENTS BEING SHARED ABOUT THE BOOK

Hello Everybody,

Look what I found...an author who is writing children's books with characters of color, Teresa Short Mitchell. Her first book is The Bathroom Tells on Me. It was selected top 8 out of 15,000 authors. She is writing a series, but needs help funding it. She incorporates curriculum standards, life and parenting skills in the book. I am donating and you can to by visiting the Go Fund Me page. If you have already purchased the book, please go to Authorhouse.com or Amazon.com and write a book review. If you would like to support her by purchasing the book, you can order it from Barnes and Nobles, Amazon.com and Authorhouse.com. It is also in ebook form. Let's get behind someone from our community who is trying to do something to help our culture, children and community.

Monica Cooper Evans

PHOTOS FROM AUTHOR-PARTICIPATING EVENTS

THE AUTHOR'S QUEST FOR SUPPORT

If you believe that the publishing industry needs more children books with characters of color, please support my efforts. My name is Teresa Short Mitchell. I am an educator of 30+ years (teacher and administrator) and I have decided to pursue my passion and dream to write children books with characters of color. I believe that God has engraved this in my heart and mind for several years. I used my own money to publish and market to the best of my ability the first in the children's book series (**The Bathroom Tells on Me**) and it was selected **top 8 out of 15,000** authors by Authorhouse Publishing. I am very proud of this accomplishment. It was also featured in **Publishers Weekly.** It is available from Amazon.com, Barnes and Nobles, and Authorhouse.com. The second book in the series is **My Report Card Tells on Me.** It has recently been released. It is my intent to deliver a heartfelt, sincere, well thought out story line for lifelong readers.

The goal of the books is to enhance, inform, enlighten and support parents, grandparents, foster parents, and guardians in their efforts to help their children develop respect and responsibility for daily life skills/ expectations. In addition, the books reinforce and support curriculum standards making it an excellent educational tool for teachers. At this time, I do not have the funds to publish and market the series; therefore, I am asking anyone reading this, valuing education and believing that the world needs purposeful children books with characters of color to please support my efforts. You can do so by donating funds (any amount will help) to a recently set up Go Fund Me account (**Books with Characters of Color**), or using your knowledge or position to assist with **FREE** publishing or marketing of the books. **I would love to have a business sponsor for this project.**

For adult readers, I have a self-published poetry book (Heartfelt Words: Words Speak When Hearts Cannot). I am willing to trade motivational speaking and/or author appearances for major assistance/support.

My website is www.tellsonmebooks.com .

Printed in the United States
By Bookmasters